Twelve Country Walks

Contents

Revised third edition compiled by Joan Deacon and published in 2009 for Isle of Wight Ramblers by Island Tourist Products Limited, Unit 7a Wootton Business Park, Whiterails Road, Wootton Bridge, Ryde, Isle of Wight PO33 4RH

ISBN 978-1-906296-07-0

Dedicated to the memory of Brian Evans. He was an enthusiastic supporter of the ideals of the Ramblers' Association, a member of the Area Council for 19 years, 10 years as our Chairman. He knew the Island intimately and through his efforts he left it a better place.

We would like to thank the Isle of Wight Council Rights of Way team for their help over the years.

1 Freshwater, Headon Warren

6½ miles

A meander through the environs of Freshwater is followed by a climb over Headon Warren with a view of the Needles and a return either on a sheltered path or over Tennyson Down. The walk starts at Moa Place, Grid Ref. 338871.

Please observe the country code, in particular keep to the footpaths, keep dogs under close control, and leave all wild flowers for others to enjoy.

Take a path leading from the side of the car park at Moa Place above the stream. This is in the direction of Brookside Road. At the road junction cross over to your right to the bridleway along Spinfish Lane.

When you reach an open grassy area go left on the grass and turn left along footpath F40 which is a field edge path. Turn right out of the field into Pound Green. (Note the Pound on your right) Turn right along Camp Road . Farringford is ahead across the fields. Turn right into Locksley Close by the post box and passing the bungalow on your left take the narrow path between houses.

Turn left up the road and at the junction go right on Bedbury Lane. Where the road bends to the left take the bridleway on the right, T7. As you reach Stonewind Farm go straight ahead through the little patch of woodland.

Go left along the road, passing St Saviour's school and church.(1) Go straight ahead at the crossroads and then bear left up hill. At the top is Christ Church. Cross the road to York Lane opposite and take second turning on the right and at the entrance to a house go left on a narrow path, T14.

Go left up the road and where it bends left take the footpath on the right. This path turns to go along the top of the cliff. Emerging from the scrub ignore the path going right and continue uphill. Passing a seat and map on your right take the right fork climbing up over Headon Warren. Pass the fenced burial mound on your left and follow the path round with views up the Solent.

Continue along the ridge with views of the Needles and at a Coast Path post go left down a steep path. This path joins a track which winds downhill. Emerging onto tarmac go left to the road into Alum Bay.(2)

St. Agnes Church Freshwater

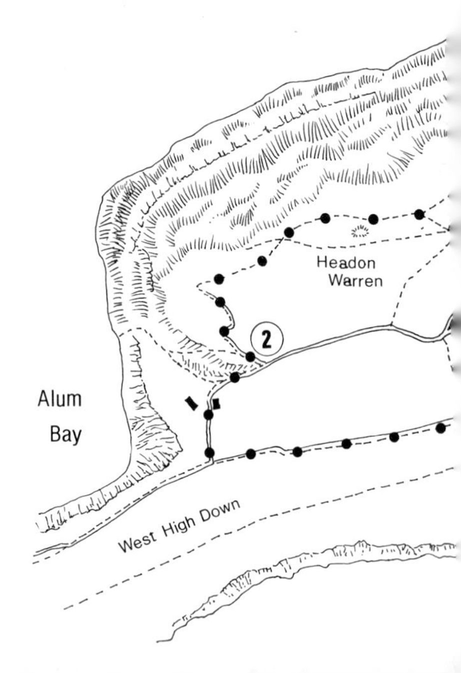

Ramble No 1

Go right along the road and then uphill past the Alum Bay attractions. Where the road to the Needles Battery turns right go left up steps. The path runs along the bottom of the down with the hedge on your left.

Passing a house away to your left and an old chalk pit on your right the path bears right towards the monument and a beacon. Over the stile by the beacon a broad grassy track leads up to the Tennyson monument.

If you are not familiar with the down it is well worth taking the route over the down for the spectacular views. As you descend towards Freshwater Bay there is a kissing gate and a low earth bank. Go left here to join the lower route.

Instead of climbing over the down follow the track forking left by the beacon. Presently you come to a crossing of paths at the top of Highdown Lane. Follow the path as it continues on the level for half a mile. The path comes into an open area by an old chalk pit. Ignore the path running off left.

Nearly half a mile further on, the scenic high level route, F72, joins the lower route just before the path emerges into fields. Bear left beside the field towards the thatched church of St Agnes.(3)

Cross the road to take the right hand of the two roads almost opposite. Go left at the crossroads along the Freshwater Way. As you approach a left hand bend go right over the stile. The path goes straight ahead, sometimes on a narrow enclosed path, reaching the road by passing close to a row of cottages.

Turn left on the road bearing right at the junction and take the footpath on your right. This crosses the playing fields and when you reach the road the car park and Moa Place is to your left.

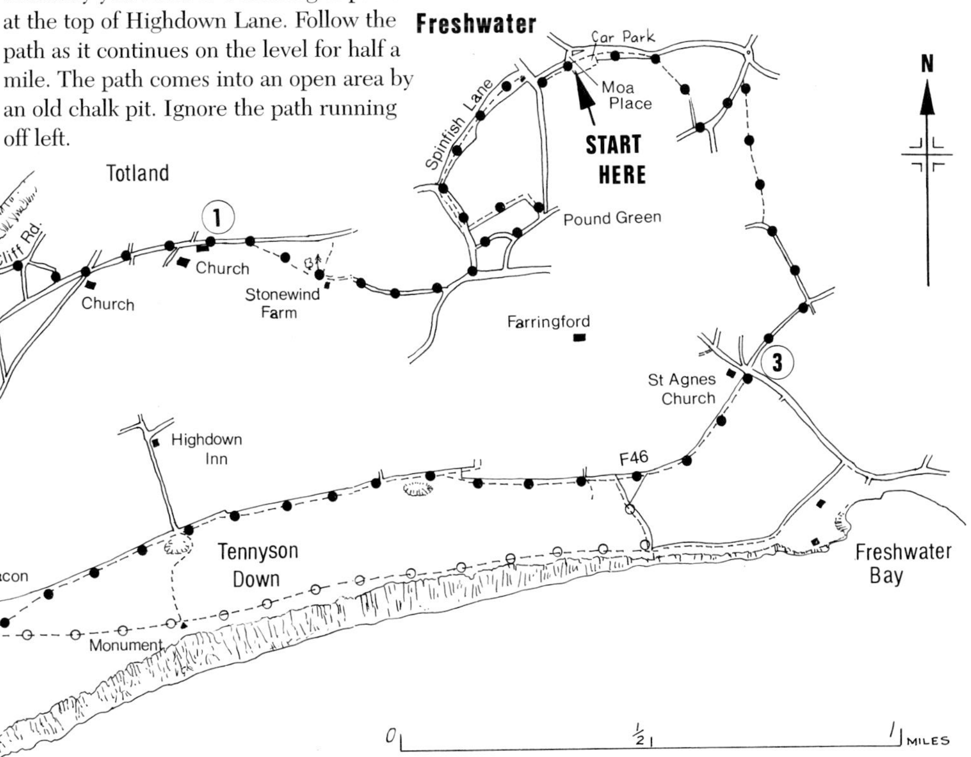

2 Yarmouth, Wellow, Tapnell and River Yar *9 miles*

An early 18th Century manor, country cottages, 'prairie' landscape and river views are included in this circular walk from Yarmouth, starting from the ferry Grid Ref. 353 897

Please observe the Country Code, in particular keep to the footpaths, keep dogs under close control, and leave wild flowers for others to enjoy.

From the ferry walk to the car park and then on the riverside path to the old mill. Turn left immediately beyond the mill on a path which joins the course of the old railway line close to what was the station building. With the station behind you cross the sluice and stile to walk on an embankment. Crossing a further stream walk ahead, passing an electricity pole on your left.

The path skirts woodland. When you reach the road go right and pass the barns of Thorley Manor. Just past the entrance take the path skirting the grounds, Y5. Continue with the trees on your left.

Bear right over the lane and cross the small field to the right of a thatched cottage. Then take a narrow path between hedges. Cross the next field walking towards the left of the farm buildings ahead. Turn right along the road and at the crossroads go left to walk along the road through the village of Thorley.

Continue on the road to Wellow ignoring the path on your right just past the Baptist Chapel. Pass the Wellow Top Road and turn right by a tiny thatched cottage. (1) This is part of the Hamstead Trail. At the top of the lane go left and then right on the bridleway. Follow this track through a wide landscape emerging at last onto Broad Lane. (2)

Bear left and then take the bridleway on the right which follows a concrete drive and then climbs between hedges. Cross the main road and continue uphill with a hedge on your left.

Just before a gate onto the open downland go right to walk with the fence on your left. At the end go through the gate and follow the path that runs along the side of the down. You shortly go through a gate into Access land. Continue with the hedge on your right. About 3/4 mile further on look for a stile on your right.

The stile and path lead you down to the left of the fence and hedge. At the bottom cross the road to the path opposite. The path goes to the right hand corner of the little wood ahead. Beyond the wood go left a short way and at the corner of the wood go diagonally right to a stile which appears to the right of some conifer trees. Over the stile walk to a gap near the left hand end of the hedge ahead.

Thorley Manor

Ramble No 2

The true line of the path is a little way from the edge of the field. You may find a path has been cleared round the edge. Passing through a shelter belt the path finally keeps to the left hand boundary to emerge through bushes onto a drive and thence to the road. (3)

Take the narrow path opposite. When you reach the road go right and as you approach the river turn right to follow the course of the old railway line back to Yarmouth.

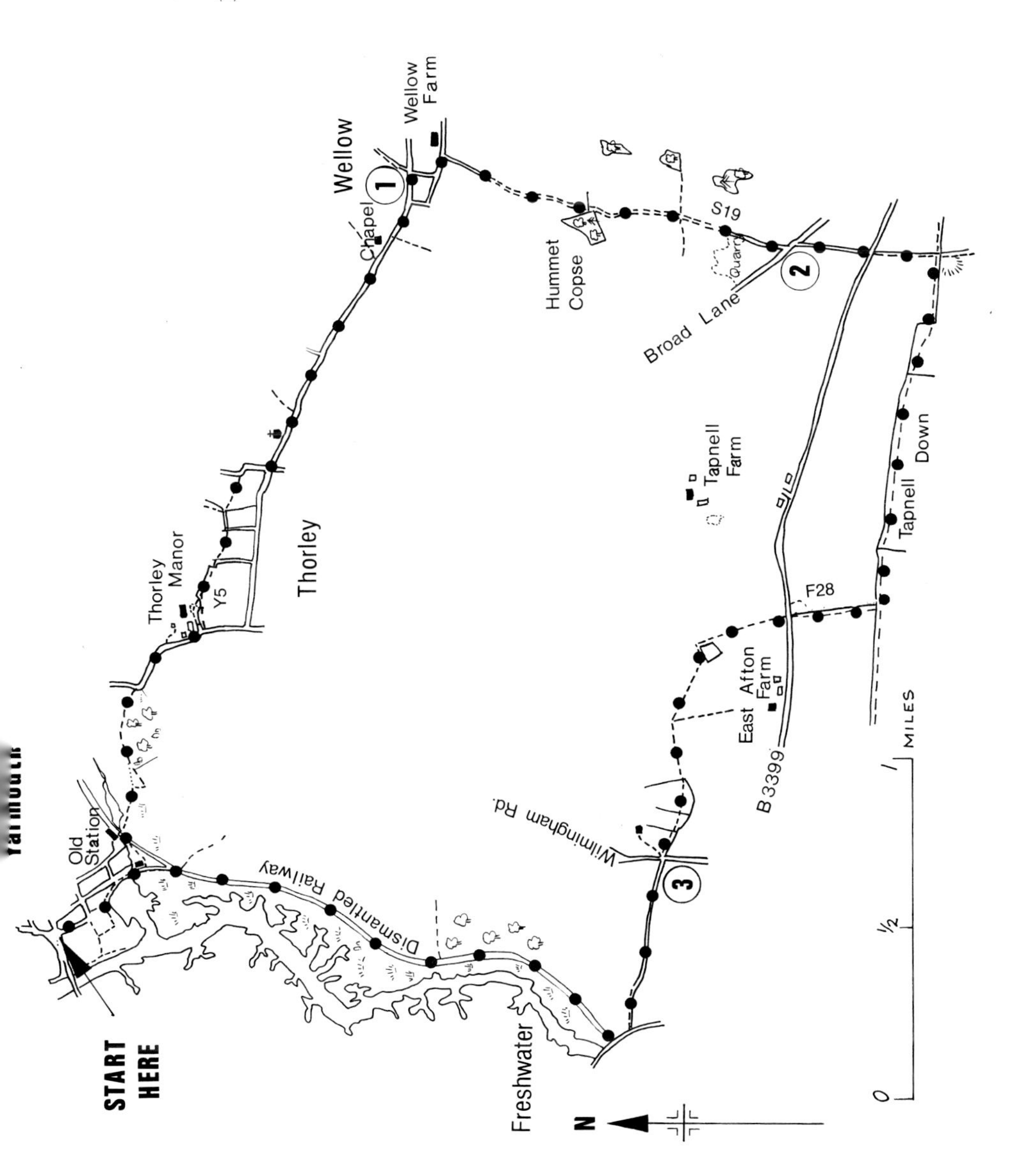

3 Yarmouth to Carisbrooke

11½ miles

This linear route takes field paths to the picturesque village of Calbourne and then climbs up onto the downs to follow the Tennyson Trail into Carisbrooke. The walk starts at the ferry terminal Grid Ref. 353897.

Please observe the country code, in particular keep to the footpaths, keep dogs under close control, and leave all wild flowers for others to enjoy.

From the ferry and buses walk south to the riverside path which is reached through the car park. Pass the tall brick building of the old mill. When you come to the track of the old railway cross over to continue on Yarmouth 1. This path enters Mill Copse.

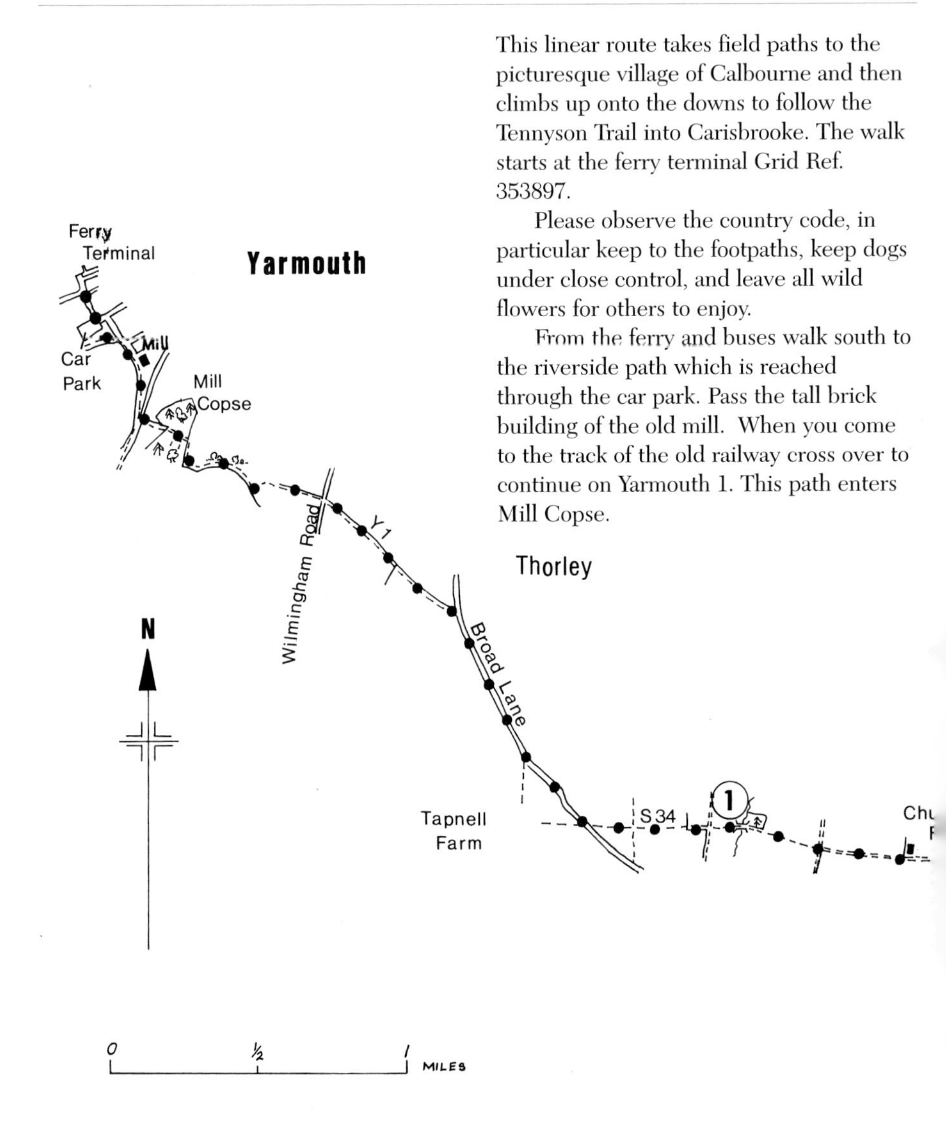

Ramble No 3

Take the path straight ahead through the copse. Leaving the copse by a gate turn right to walk on the field edge. Round to the left the path in a little while goes between hedges. Regaining the field edge the path presently goes up left towards the remnant of a hedge. Walk with the hedge on your left.

Cross the lane and continue with the hedge on your left. When you reach Broad Lane turn right to walk for nearly a mile along it.

Turn left leaving the road where a guide post indicates the path. A short distance ahead a guide post at a crossing of paths shows the path ahead. (The television mast at Rowridge is straight ahead in the distance.)

Presently descend, to a bridge at the corner of a copse. (1) Climb the field beside the copse and on up across the field. There is a round white marker beside a stile at a crossing of paths.

The path continues ahead passing Churchills Farm and eventually emerging onto the road.

Turn left to reach a path almost opposite which runs inside the field. This path descends the field and runs along the bottom edge to a stile in the far corner. Cross the stile into the wood bearing left to walk gently downhill. Over a stile the path goes through a marshy area under a line of electricity poles.

The path goes on beside the stream through several fields below Eades Farm. Leaving the last field turn sharp right to climb up round a cottage. Follow the edge of the field round behind the cottage. Take the path across the field. The path goes down steps among trees and bushes. Bear left to reach a footbridge. At the other side climb the steps and at a junction of paths go left to the road (Normans Corner).

Turn right to walk along the road and where the guide post indicates turn right, CB13. Go straight ahead between the bushes and at the far side cross the stile on your left into a field. Calbourne Mill is down to your right.

bridge

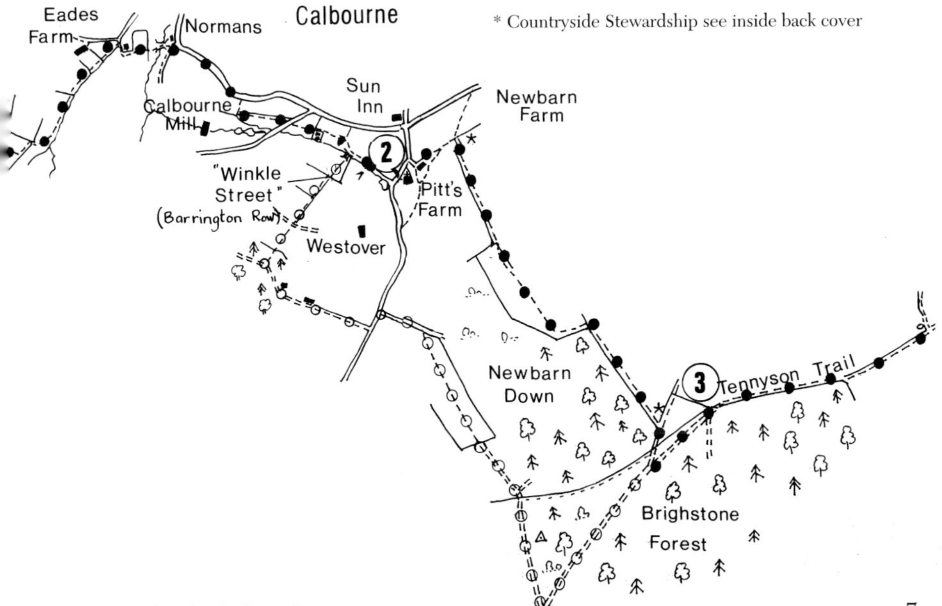

Eades Farm
Normans
Calbourne
Sun Inn
Newbarn Farm
Calbourne Mill
"Winkle Street"
(Barrington Row)
Westover
Pitt's Farm
Newbarn Down
Tennyson Trail
Brighstone Forest

* Countryside Stewardship see inside back cover

The path runs beside the hedge. Across the road climb the steps to follow the path through three fields. In the third field descend to the stile in the far corner and walk beside the stream up through Winkle Street. Turn left up along the road through the village of Calbourne.

The village pump is under a triangular roof. Turn right here (2) and left in front of the farmhouse. The path passes the grassy pit and crosses the field towards two stiles. *Over the right hand one turn right to walk with the fence on your right. Presently cross to walk with the fence on your left and then continue ahead . The path descends towards the fence and then goes left to a gate by the corner of the forest. Through the gate go right to walk beside the fence on a path which climbs steeply.

Where this path ends * turn right to follow the track which leads into the forest . In 100 metres turn sharp left onto the Tennyson Trail.

Leaving the forest (3) the path goes along the side of a field with an old hedge and the forest on your right presently going through a gate to continue in the same direction with the hedge on your left.

Continuing in the same general direction follow the well defined path which is the Tennyson Trail and which leads leads into Nodgham Lane in Carisbrooke.

Bear left to reach the High Street. Go right down hill to reach the centre of the village.

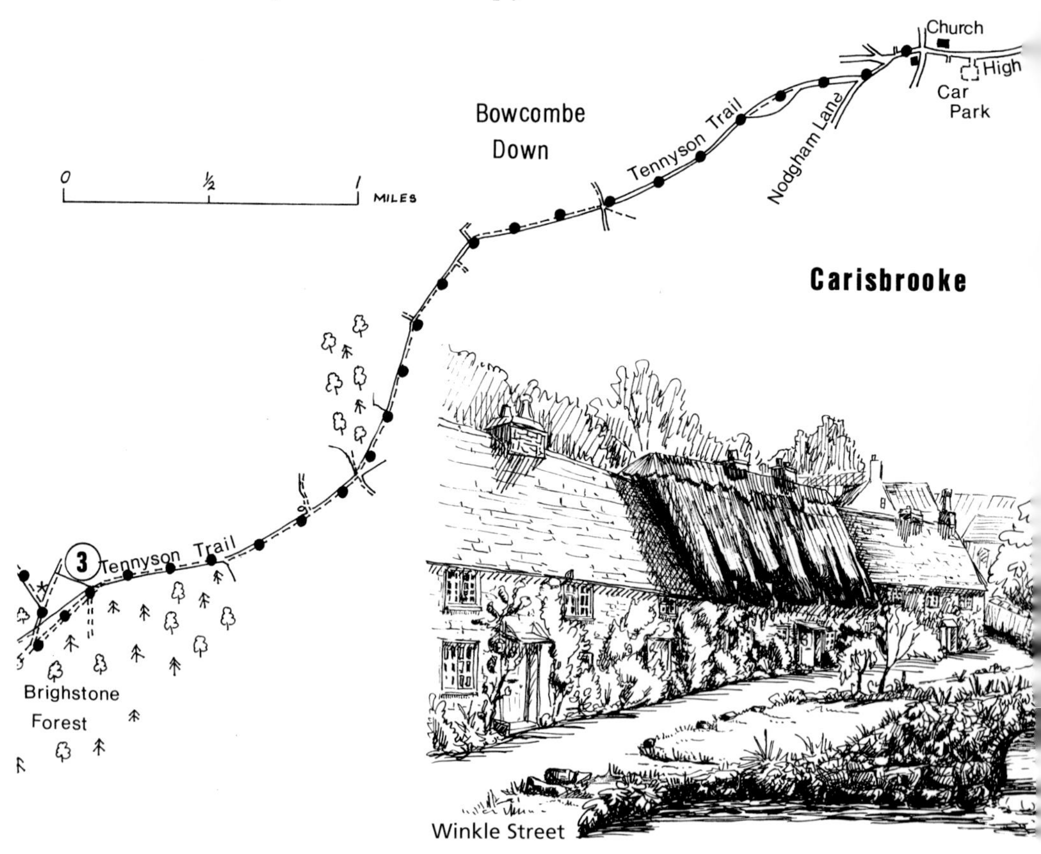

4 Newport to Sandown

9 miles

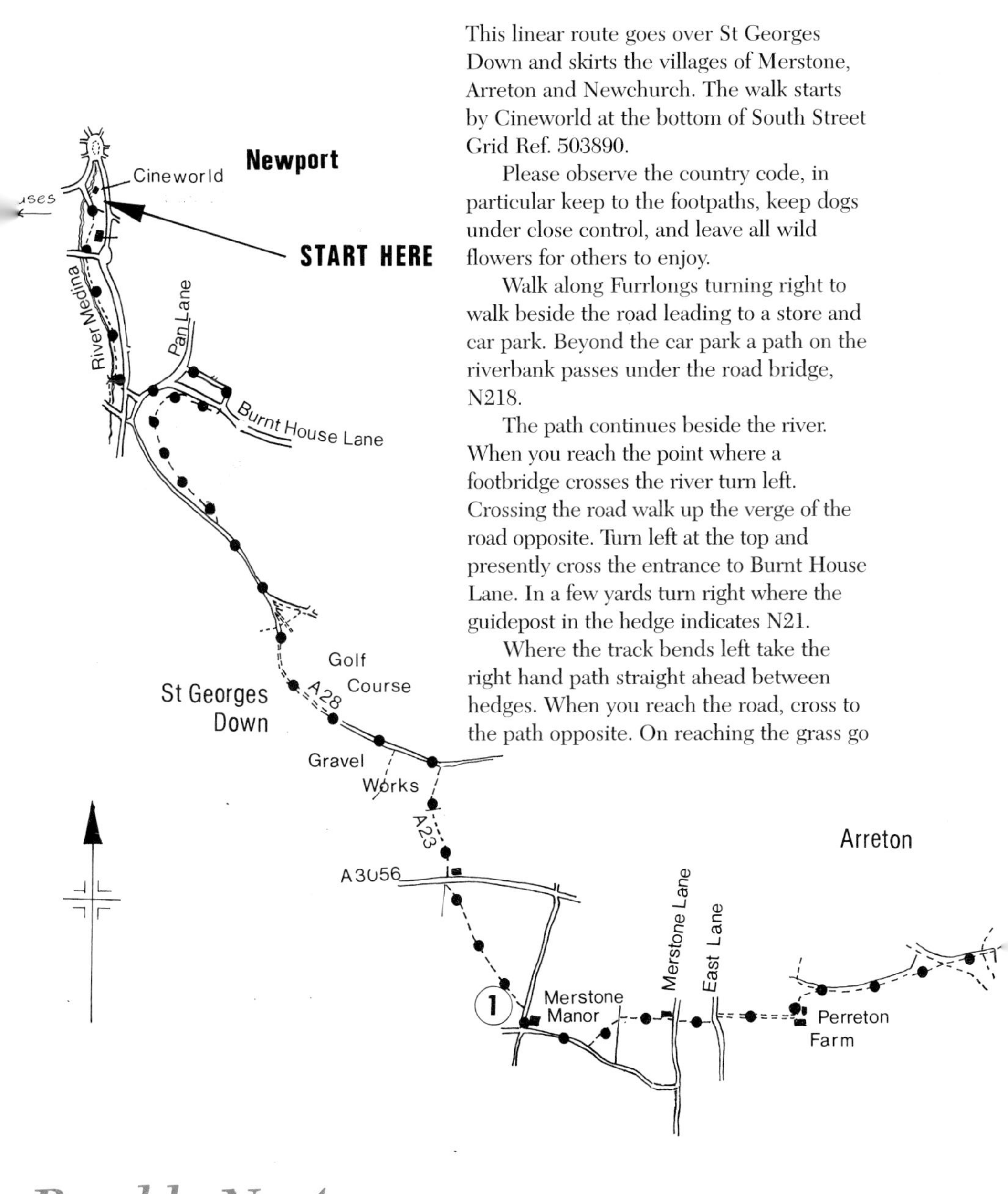

This linear route goes over St Georges Down and skirts the villages of Merstone, Arreton and Newchurch. The walk starts by Cineworld at the bottom of South Street Grid Ref. 503890.

Please observe the country code, in particular keep to the footpaths, keep dogs under close control, and leave all wild flowers for others to enjoy.

Walk along Furrlongs turning right to walk beside the road leading to a store and car park. Beyond the car park a path on the riverbank passes under the road bridge, N218.

The path continues beside the river. When you reach the point where a footbridge crosses the river turn left. Crossing the road walk up the verge of the road opposite. Turn left at the top and presently cross the entrance to Burnt House Lane. In a few yards turn right where the guidepost in the hedge indicates N21.

Where the track bends left take the right hand path straight ahead between hedges. When you reach the road, cross to the path opposite. On reaching the grass go

Ramble No 4

right to presently look out across Newport. Go left up the hill and over the brow follow the edge of the down round to the left. Presently a gap gives access to the lane beyond the hedge. Continue uphill on the lane.

At the top of the hill take the right hand track (Bembridge Trail) which runs along the top of the down between gorse bushes with the golf course on your left and presently the gravel quarry on your right.

Ignore the path on your right which goes through the quarry. At the end of the gravel workings cross the stile on your right to walk beside the hedge on your right to the next stile where there is an extensive view. The white tower of Newchurch church is away to your left.

Descend the steps and follow the path downhill emerging onto to road to the right of some cottages. Across the road the path goes diagonally left across a large field. At the far side turn right on the lane to Merstone Manor.(1) At the crossing of tracks go left.

As you come to the end of the farm buildings on your right go diagonally left on a path across the field, crossing a newly made farm track. There is a stile in the hedge just to the left of the trees. Walk ahead and pass to the right of a house and garden.

Cross straight over the lane. At the second lane take the path along the access track to Perreton Farm. In the farmyard turn left leaving the farmyard through a double gate. Bear right to walk on the left hand side of a little valley.

Where the path begins to descend go through the gate and another on your right. The path descends to a little bridge and you walk again on the left hand side of the valley.

In the corner at the far end of this pasture cross the stile, cross a narrow field and pass beside a garden to reach the main road. Turn right and then cross the road to go along the lane to Heasley Manor.(2) Just before the car park turn right. Cross the footbridge and take the path straight ahead.

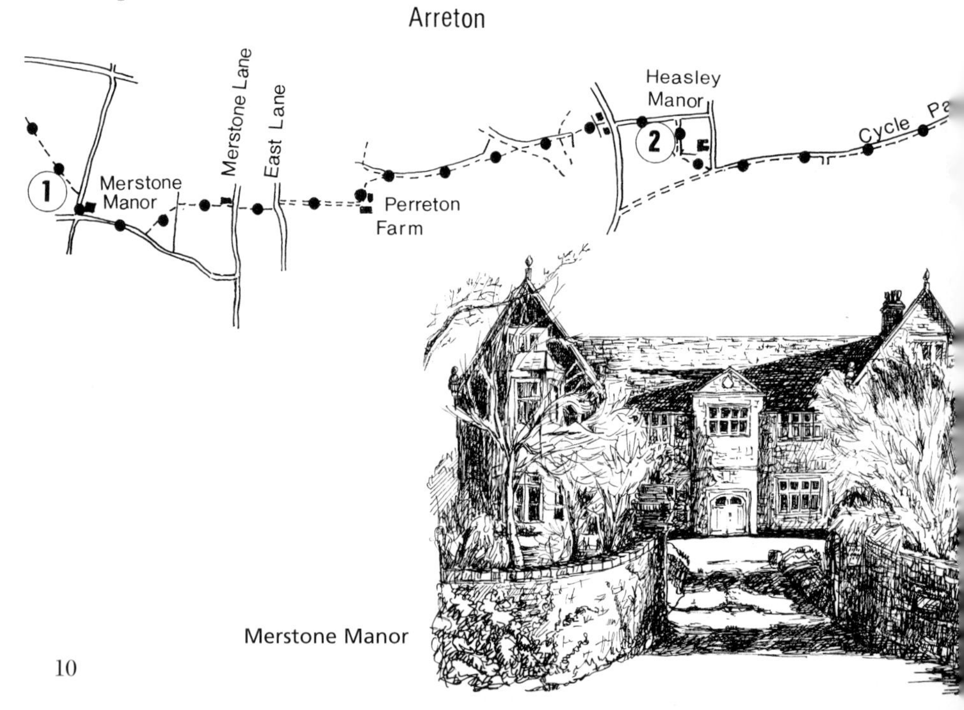

Merstone Manor

Turn left on the old railway line and follow it to Langbridge.

When you reach the road turn right. At the entrance to Parsonage Farm on the left take the track that leads up towards the church.(3) A little path near the top leads into the churchyard (snowdrops and crocuses). You can rejoin the track a few metres further on.

The track runs beside the churchyard and then beside a field. A guide post indicates a path at right angles. Cross the field, recently planted with trees, turning left when you reach the hedge. At the bottom of the field the path descends to cross a footbridge and then bears right to climb the other side.

At the top of the hill cross the track with Hill Farm on your left and descend the track and then a path. Over the little stream the path ascends to presently go between fences uphill along the back of gardens.

The path emerges on the corner of a road. Almost immediately take a path in the field on your right to walk beside the hedge. At the top of the second field cross the two roads into Burnt House Lane and shortly turn right down a sunken way.

At the bottom turn left to walk beside the fence and then on a boardwalk. At the junction of boardwalks go right to reach the woodland.

Take the path going left along the edge of the wood beside the stream. Turn right along the track. When you reach the road bear right passing the water works on your left.

Take the road which passes between the school playing fields and where it bends right go straight ahead beside a triangle of green. Cross the road to go through the subway and go left to reach the station. Station Avenue leads to the town centre and at the bottom bear right and then left into the High Street for the buses.

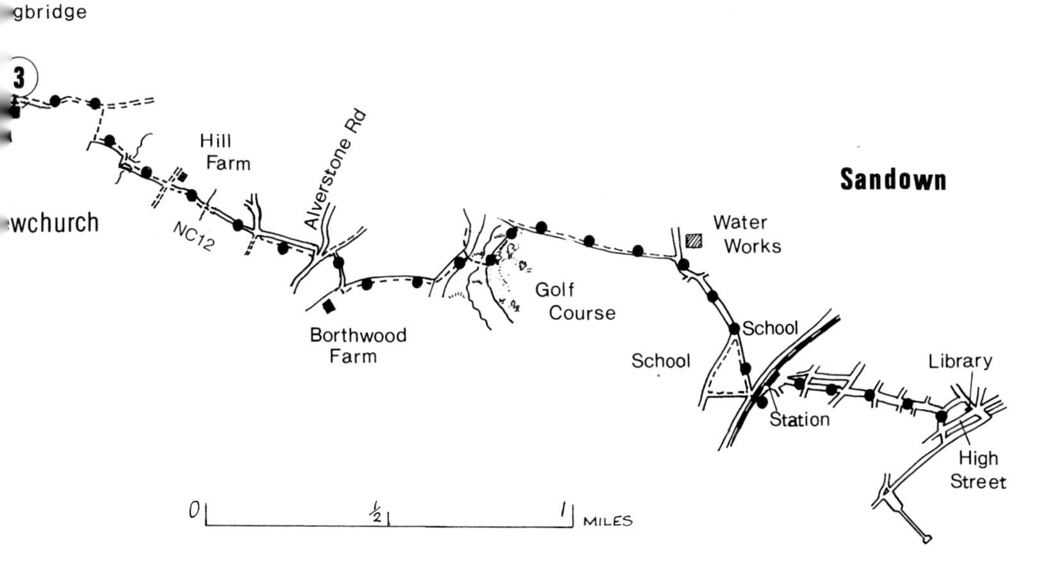

5 Newport, Gunville, Bowcombe Down, Plaish *6 miles*

From the centre of Newport this walk follows field paths, climbs up onto the downs and returns via the village of Carisbrooke.

Please observe the country code, in particular keep to the footpaths, keep dogs under close control, and leave all wild flowers for others to enjoy.

The walk starts at the Post Office in the High Street. Go along Post Office Lane, which leads away from the High Street beside the Post Office. Walk across the car park and turn left at the bottom. Go right with the road and take the footpath ahead, N211. You shortly leave the tarmac to walk between hedges. (A planned development here means that just before joining Petticoat Lane the route will go left along a new road for a short distance and then right to join the Lane – a footpath between hedges.)

Presently cross a road and continue ahead. Through the gate walk in the field with the hedge on your left presently descending to cross a bridge and continue with the fence on your right up to the corner of the field. Through the gate walk with the hedge on your right.

Leaving this field go left and follow the path between bushes to walk through the next fields with the stream out of sight on your left.

Turn left along the road to take the first turning on the right - Ash Lane. (1) Cross the stile and bear left to the corner of the field and bear right over the footbridge and stile. Walk with the hedge and ditch on your left.

Leaving the field go straight ahead on the farm track, Poleclose Farm, presently turning to pass a converted barn on your left. In a short while go left with the hedge on your right. Continue in the same direction across the fields ahead, bearing slightly right and passing a big oak tree, to the corner where a stile gives access to a farm track. Turn left by farm buildings.

At the entrance to Cooks Farm bear right walking with a ditch on your left. Go round with the track, through the farm yard passing the barns and Read's farmhouse on your right. Go through the gate ahead turn right and then left on a chalk track up hill. Round the corner half way up look for a stile on your left and climb to the road.

Turn right along the road towards the Blacksmiths Arms. (2) Turn left opposite the public house onto the bridleway N197.

Blacksmith's Arms

Ramble No 5

In a short while take the left hand fork to climb with the hedge on your left.

Descending the down on the other side you come to a meeting of paths. Go into the field to the left of the track ahead. The path, N126, goes diagonally left and presently a double stile comes into view about halfway down the hedge-line on your left.

Over the stile the path descends, more steeply now, to just left of a blue 'dead end' road sign visible on the roadside.

Cross the road to go down the lane opposite and just in front of Plaish Farm (3) go right. The grassy track meets another track. Bear left here and presently go left across a stile to walk with the hedge on your right and the Lukely Brook on your left, towards Carisbrooke Castle.

The path leaves the final field across a footbridge. Turn right up the lane and take the first lane on your left. This is Millers Lane and you presently see the tower of the church straight ahead.

The lane swings round to the left. Walk beside the ford (4) and up towards the church. At the main road cross to the right to climb steps into the churchyard. Turn right to walk beside a brick wall and along the path ahead leaving the churchyard. Where paths meet by the pond turn right to walk with a school playing field on your left.

As you approach the school building look for a path on your right. This path passes a primary school on your left. Cross the road to the path opposite and at the end of this path go straight ahead along Wilver Road and then Westminster Lane.

At the end of Westminster Lane go on along the road to the end, turning right and then left along Crocker Street to cross the car park to the Post Office Lane and the start of the walk.

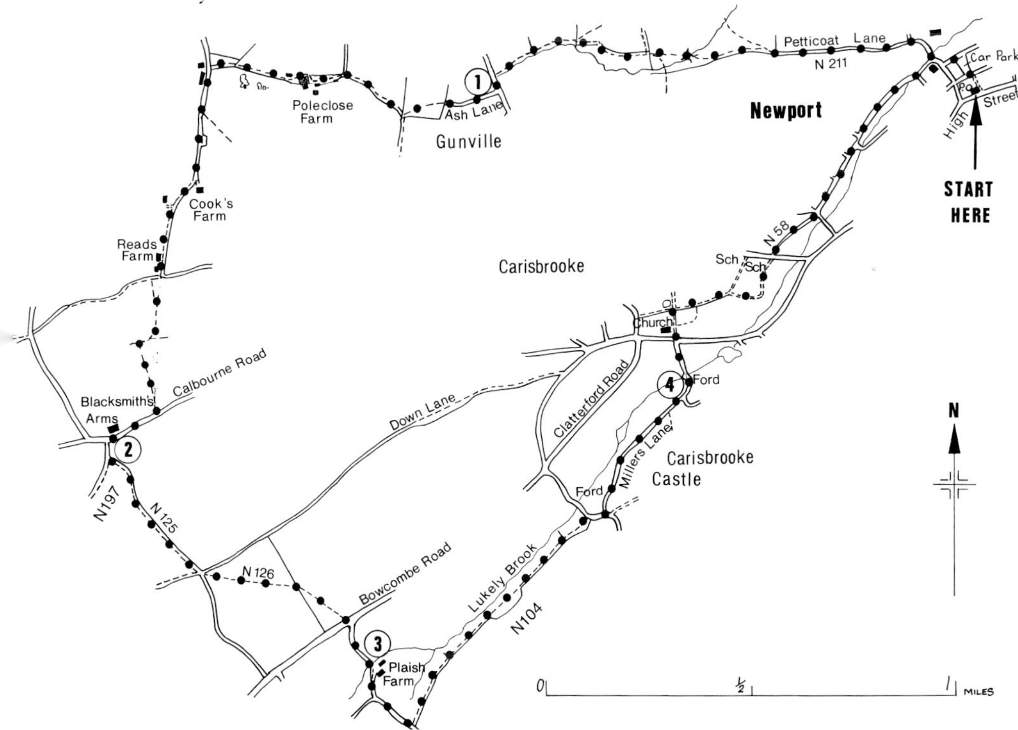

6 Newport Quay, New Fairlee, Binfield, River Medina *4½ or 6 miles*

Field paths, woodland and a riverside walk are encountered on this walk from Newport Quay Grid Ref. 501894.

Please observe the country code, in particular keep to the footpaths, keep dogs under close control, and leave all wild flowers for others to enjoy.

The walk starts from the quay in Newport. Walk under the road bridge and immediately turn right to walk with the Riverside Centre on your left. Past the car park walk up the slope and go through the tunnel. You are on the old Newport to Ryde railway line.

Follow the path along this track, crossing Halberry Lane, to Mews Lane. Turn right on N118 towards New Fairlee Farm. The track passes Little Fairlee Farm and continues between hedges, presently bearing right. When the farm buildings come into sight continue beside the field with the hedge on your left. Passing the buildings on your right, you come to a meeting of paths. (1)

Turn left to follow N116 with the hedge on your left. Walk in this direction by several fields leaving the last one by a stile in the corner to the left of a pylon. (2) A path straight ahead leads down to the access track to Belmont Farm and goes under the old railway bridge to reach the A3054. (3) (There is a fine viewpoint at the next stile.)

The path to the right makes the walk a little longer. Take the path descending gently through woodland. At the bottom of the slope, where the field on your right becomes woodland turn to walk along the path to the left.

Go through the gate onto the old railway line. Turn left passing the buildings of what was Whippingham station on your right. About 30 metres before a fence across the track a path goes down the embankment on the right. Turn right to reach the A3054. (3)

Cross the main road with care and walk down the road opposite to Island Harbour and straight ahead to the riverside.

Passing the control tower on your right turn left along the old millpond wall with the paddle steamer Ryde Queen on your left. Follow the riverside path into Newport.

As you reach Newport Harbour and the Travel Inn the path continues beside the fence on your right behind the warehouses. Walk along the Quay towards the road bridge and the Riverside Centre.

Ryde Queen as she was

Ramble No 6

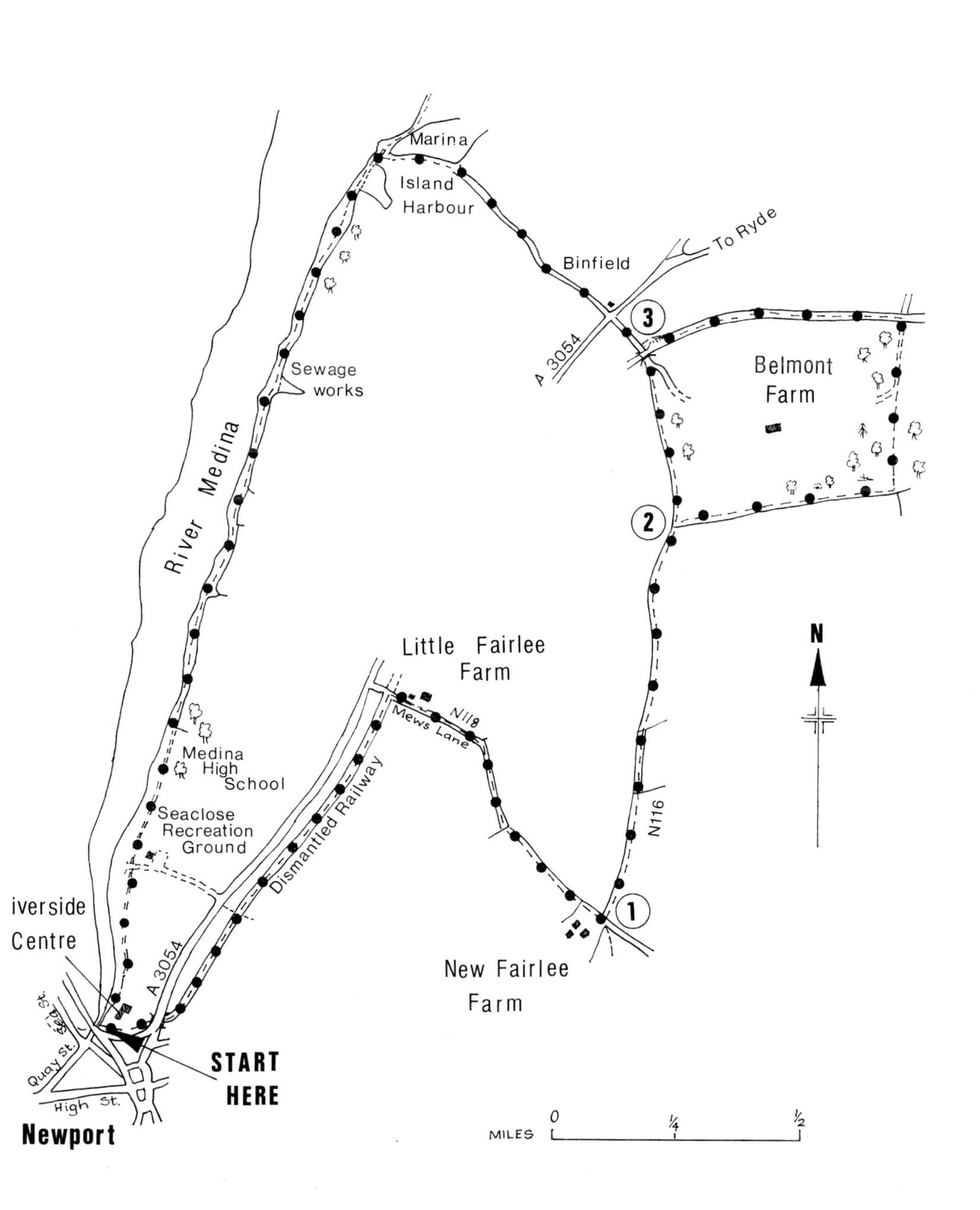
Marina
Island
Harbour
To Ryde
Binfield
3
A 3054
Belmont
Farm
Sewage
works
River Medina
2
N
Little Fairlee
Farm
N118
Mews Lane
Medina
High
School
Dismantled Railway
N116
Seaclose
Recreation
Ground
iverside
Centre
1
A 3054
New Fairlee
Farm
Sea St.
Quay St.
START
HERE
High St.
Newport
0
¼
½
MILES

7 Newport, St George's Down, Merstone Manor *7½ miles*

This walk explores the countryside to the south of Newport passing two Manors on the way. The walk starts at the bottom of South Street by Cineworld. Grid Ref. 503890.

Please observe the country code, in particular keep to the footpaths, keep dogs under close control, and leave all wild flowers for others to enjoy.

Walk along Furrlongs passing KFC on your left. Cross the road at the crossing and continue up Furrlongs. Take the second turning on the right, Home Mead, and passing three pairs of semi-detatched houses on the right, go along the footpath, N9, beside the gate to the allotments.

The path presently crosses a footbridge and skirts the football field. Turn right in Pan Lane and then go left where a guide post indicates N40. This track goes towards Little Pan Farm. Past the farm you come to a crossing of tracks where you turn right. Cross Burnt House Lane and climb through fields towards Garretts Farm. (1)

At the farm pass the house on your right. At the corner of the property turn left to go downhill. You leave the farm area on a grassy track.

Go down to the gate and continue ahead. This is part of the golf course. There is a waymark on a big oak tree on your right. Halfway down the slope bear right towards the stile on the edge of the wood.

Cross the stile to walk along the left hand edge of the wood. Continue along the hedge line until you reach a track coming down from the right. Go left past a ruined building and down the field with the trees and ditch on your right.

Over the footbridge at the bottom cross the field ahead climbing steeply, presently walking with the hedge on your left. Over the top of the hill cross the stile to descend an enclosed path. Emerging into a field, go down to the left hand corner by Great East Standen Manor.

Cross the two stiles here and follow the hedge round, ignoring the gates into the farm, to a stile opposite a brick house. Turn right up the lane.

Passing the Manor bear left through gates on the track. At the top at a meeting of paths go right between hedges on A28. In a while the path begins to descend and the gravel pit works come into view. Look out for a guide post on the left indicating Bridleway A29. Go down here to the main road towards Merstone.

At the bottom cross the road to walk down the lane to Merstone Manor.(2) At the cross roads of tracks by the Manor go straight ahead.

The concrete track crosses the line of the old railway, now a cycleway to your left. Presently you turn right on the bridleway/cycleway. Passing a house on your left the way becomes a metalled track. A short distance past houses and barns on your left a guide post indicates the cycleway turning right. Follow this, crossing the road at Blackwater and continuing to Shide.

At the end of the track cross the road to Shide Path opposite. Presently turn right along a narrow path to cross the footbridge. Go left along the riverbank passing under a road and skirting the car park at the superstore to return to the start.

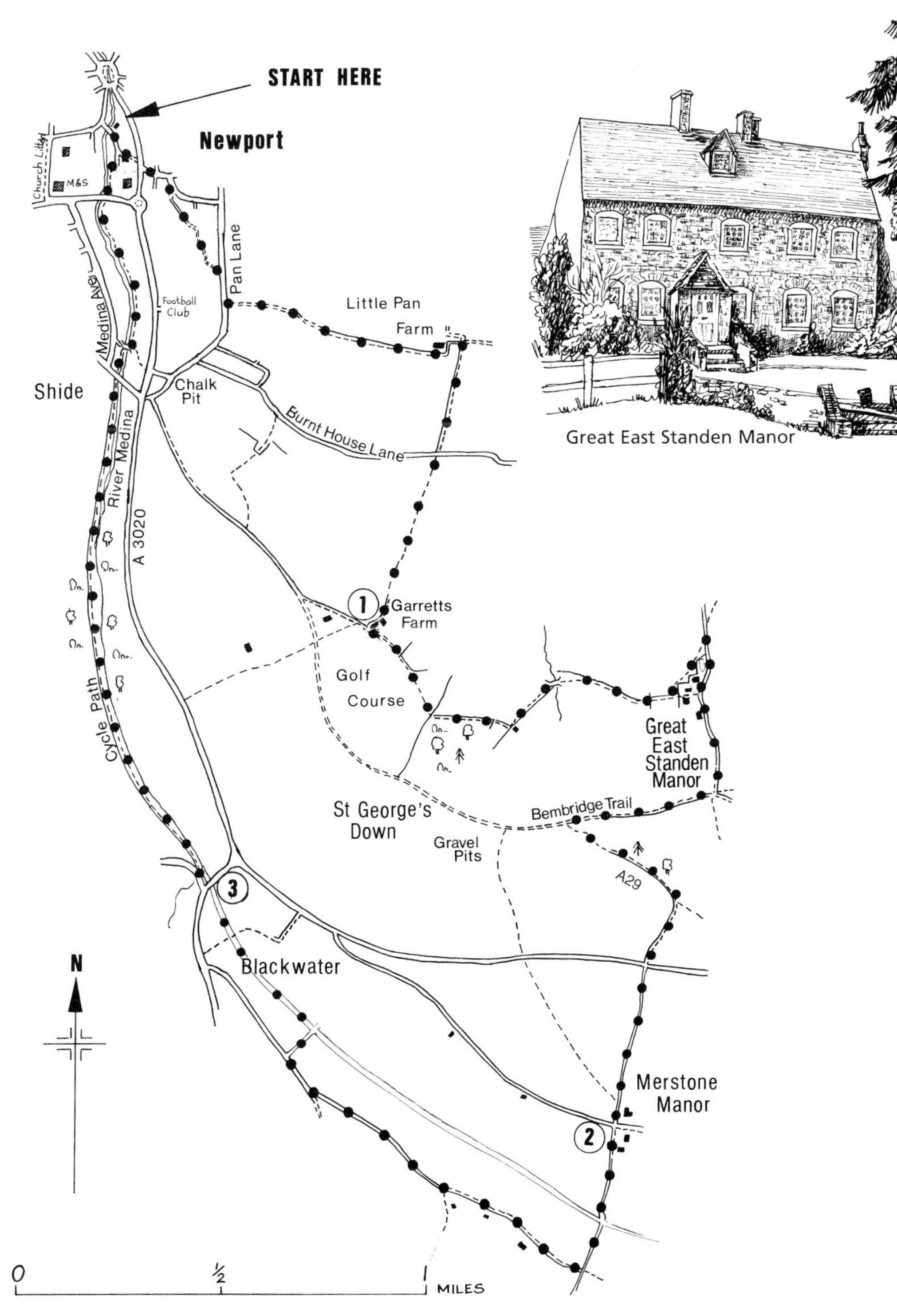

Great East Standen Manor

8 Wootton, Littletown, Woodhouse Farm *3 miles*

A short walk through countryside to the south of Wootton this route starts at the car park near the shops in the village Grid Ref. 544920.

Please observe the country code, in particular keep to the footpaths, keep dogs under close control, and leave all wild flowers for others to enjoy.

The walk starts in Brannon Way which is just below the supermarket in Wootton High Street and on the opposite side. Walk along Brannon Way away from the High Street and turn right to go up Mary Rose Avenue. Continue up curving left and right, Mary Rose Avenue becomes Fernside Way and at the top Fernhill. At the 'T' junction turn left into Station Road and in a few metres bear left along Packsfield Lane.

This track crosses the Isle of Wight (steam) Railway Line. (1) Over the crossing bear left up a narrow bridleway. Passing Woodford Cottage continue up to the top of the Bridleway.

At the top turn left as far as the corner then follow the track which bends to the right passing the house on your left. Just past a cottage on your right turn left over a stile. Walking with the line of trees in the middle of the field on your right, go towards the stile.

The path passes between two electricity poles to the next stile and then to the corner of a wood. At the top of the wood bear right with the hedge on your right to a stile in the corner.

Over the stile go left. In a few metres turn left on a track which avoids the farmyard.

The path leads down to cross the railway line again (2) and continues, bearing left on a well defined track between hedges. Follow this track as it meanders back to Wootton.

With the creek on your right you reach Wootton High Street just above the bridge. Turn left uphill passing shops to Brannon Way.

Woodhouse Farm

Ramble No 8

Wootton Bridge

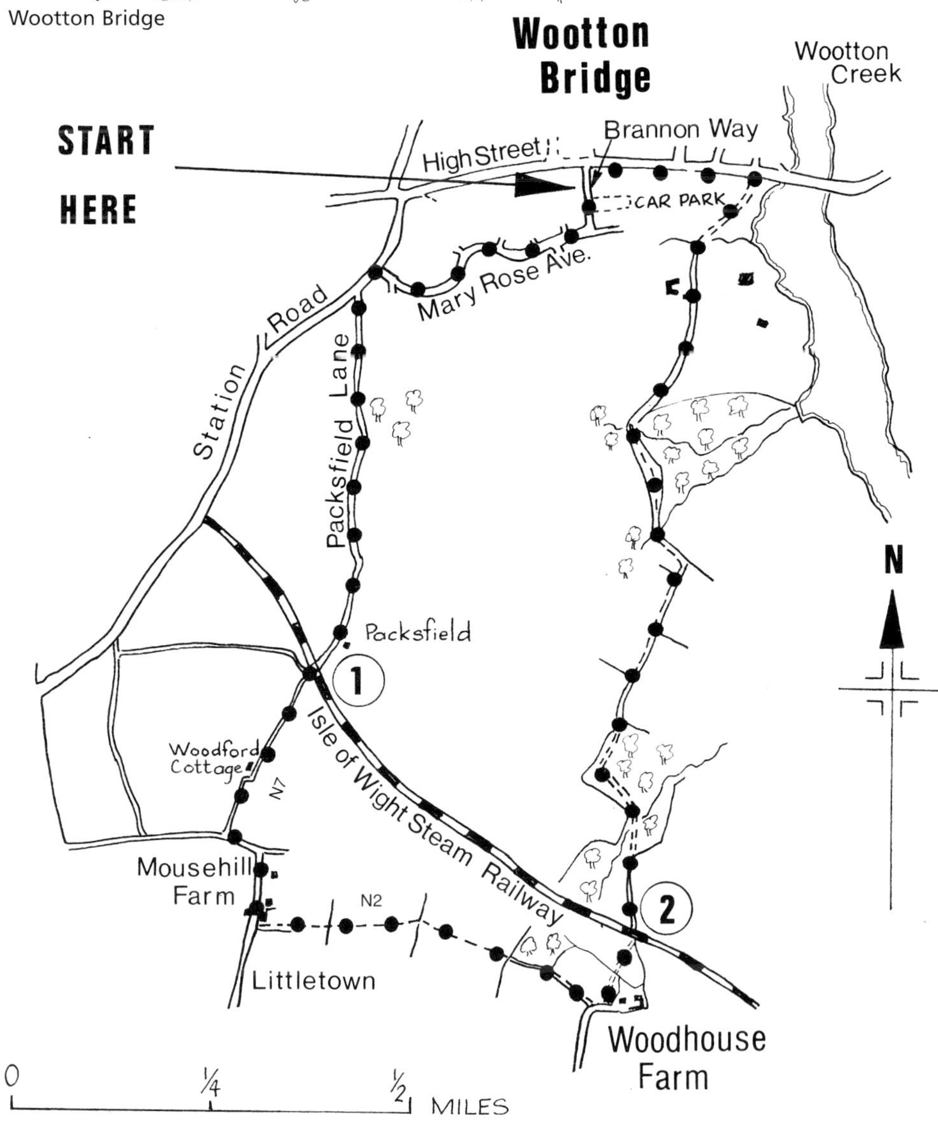

9 Ryde, Binstead, Dame Anthony's Common *5 miles*

Leaving the western outskirts of Ryde the walk passes the ruins of Quarr Abbey and returns via field paths and residential streets. The walk starts at Ryde pier Grid Ref. 594929.

Please observe the country code, in particular keep to the footpaths, keep dogs under close control, and leave all wild flowers for others to enjoy.

At the entrance to Ryde Pier turn to walk with the sea on your right. Follow the road partly round the roundabout into St Thomas' Street. Passing the car park on your left turn right into Buckingham Road, presently turning left uphill. Turn right into Spencer Road and continue up to its end.

Go through the metal barrier and go diagonally right into R48, 'Ladies' Walk', which crosses a golf course. At the bottom by the bridge a short path leads down to the sea. (1) Back at the bridge continue up the hill to Binstead Church.

Leaving the church turn right along Church Road and go right into bridleway R45 turning left at big gateposts. At the end of this path turn right down the road.

Through the gate there are views of brick built Quarr Abbey on the hill and the remains of the old abbey below. At Quarr Abbey Farm turn left. (2)

Cross the road to the path opposite and walk with the hedge on your right. Near the end of the field go right to follow the path through the wood. As you leave the trees a stile leads to a path up across the field towards houses on the skyline. Turn left along Newnham Lane to Bartons Corner.

Cross the road ahead bearing left to the next corner. Go along the narrow path R41, on your right, which runs along behind bungalows. This becomes a path between hedges. Follow this path round, ignoring path R113 on the left to reach an open area with young oak trees. (3)

Turn left to walk with the hedge on your left. Just before the gate at the bottom turn left through a kissing gate. (An option here is to go through the gate, up the track a short distance, left under the arch into Play Lane Millenium Green. Passing the stone compass, fork left to follow the path which winds down to cross the stream. Go left to rejoin the main route.)

At a junction of paths take the middle path, climbing through trees. The path curves right and then left behind houses. Cross the road, Hillside Avenue, (4) and continue roughly parallel with the stream. At the end of the path go left to Binstead Lodge Road. Go right here and then left to cross an open area of grass to the mini roundabout on the main road. Cross the road to R49 which presently crosses the golf course to Ladies Walk. Follow the outward route to return to Ryde Pier.

Quarr Abbey Ruins

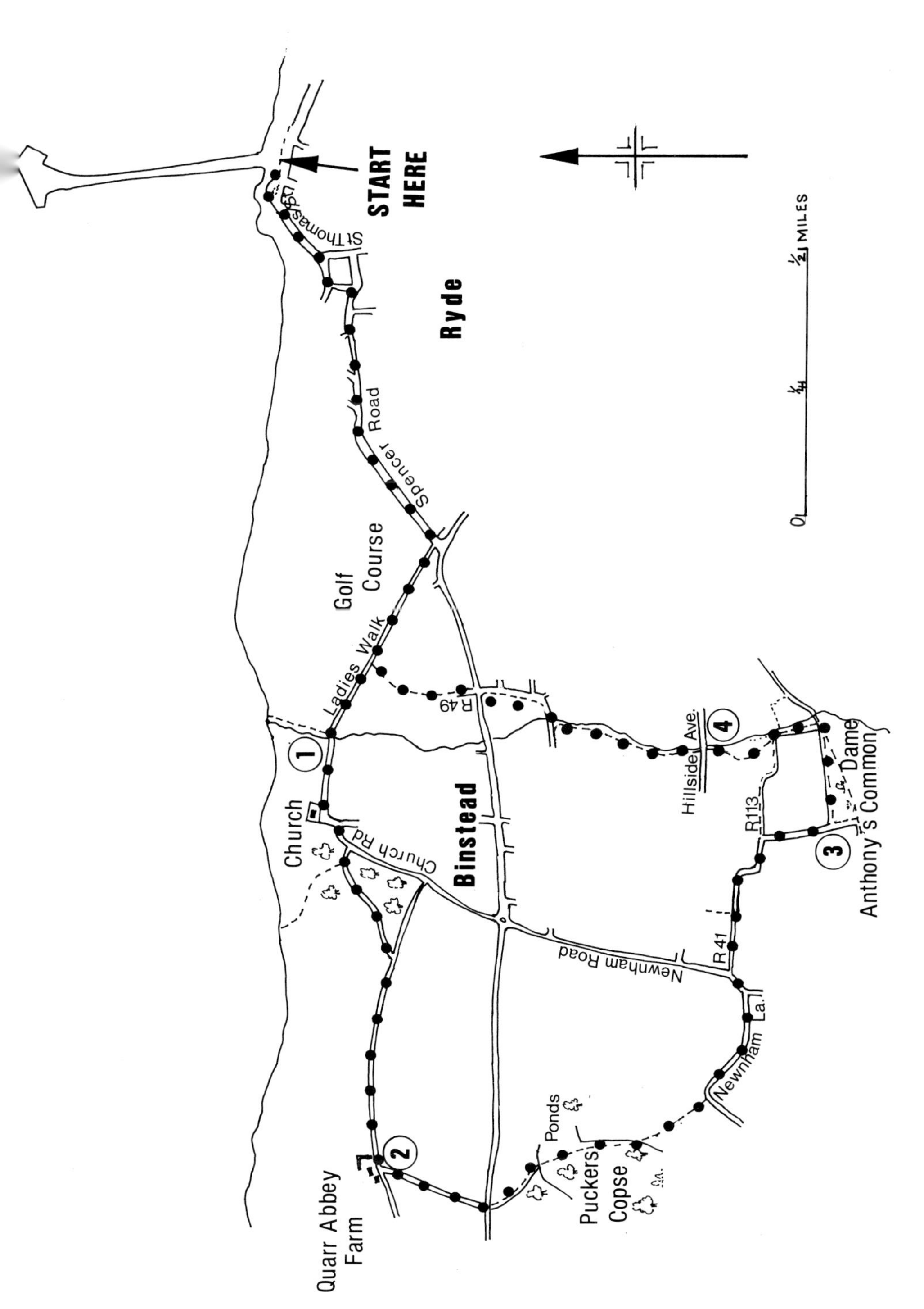
START HERE
St Thomas St.
Ryde
Spencer Road
Golf Course
Ladies Walk
R49
1
Church
Church Rd
Binstead
Hillside Ave.
4
R113
Dame Anthony's Common
3
R41
Newnham Road
Newnham La.
Ponds
Puckers Copse
2
Quarr Abbey Farm
0
¼
½ MILES

10 Brading, Alverstone, Sandown Marsh *7½ miles*

This walk from The Bull Ring in the centre of Brading can also start from the station. It climbs the side of the down and then descends to meander through lowland by the River Yar. Start from the Bull Ring Grid Ref: 606870 (or from the station.)

Please observe the Country Code, in particular keep to footpaths, keep dogs under close control, and leave all wild flowers for others to enjoy.

From the Bull Ring walk up The Mall to bridleway B39, on the right. Passing Little Jane's Cottage, the path, lined by trees, rises along the lower slope of the down.

Take the path on the right indicated by a yellow waymark. At a meeting of paths continue ahead. Presently in a chalk pit on the left is a wooden carved memorial. Nunwell House can be glimpsed through the trees on the right.

As you approach the end of the trees, go through the bridle gate and in a short while take the right hand fork. This grassy path curves gently left presently joining a track coming up on your right. This leads up to a gate. Through the gate turn right to walk beside the hedge up to the road. (1).

Turn right to walk along the verge. After the sharp bend in the road cross to descend a grassy track B33. At Kern Farm the path goes to the left of the farm and then ahead down the lane.

On a sharp bend go straight ahead over a stile. At the next corner continue ahead and then left on a track to the road (Alverstone). Turn right and over the bridge look for a path on your left, NC17. (2)

The path crosses boardwalks and ascends to go through a wood. Leaving the wood near the bird hide go left down the track. At the bend go straight ahead through the kissing gate and then straight over the cycle path. Bear right over bridges and stiles. Presently go through a gate and up to a second gate. Turn right before the gate to walk with the hedge on your left. The path curves left to reach the road.

Go right and turn down the first turning on the right. Over the bridge go left on a path beside the stream * When you come to a footbridge go right with the fence on your right. Near the end of this field the path goes left to cross the bridge.

In the field go left to walk along the bottom of three fields. At the end go down steps to the footbridge. (3) The path leads ahead across the marsh. Over the second bridge the path goes left and then right across low lying land to walk up a narrow field with the hedge on your right.

Over stile the path continues straight ahead and then climbs with the hedge on your right to the corner of the field. An enclosed path leads to the road.

Go right and past the houses take a path on your right which climbs across the field. At the far side go down steps to the road. Go right along the road and at the junction continue to the traffic lights. Cross straight over and at the railway bridge ahead go left down steps to walk beside the track.

Just before the station cross the track and follow the path, keeping right, to the road, Station Road. Go left along it and at the end, straight ahead to reach the Bull Ring.

* Countryside Stewardship see inside back cover

Ramble No 10

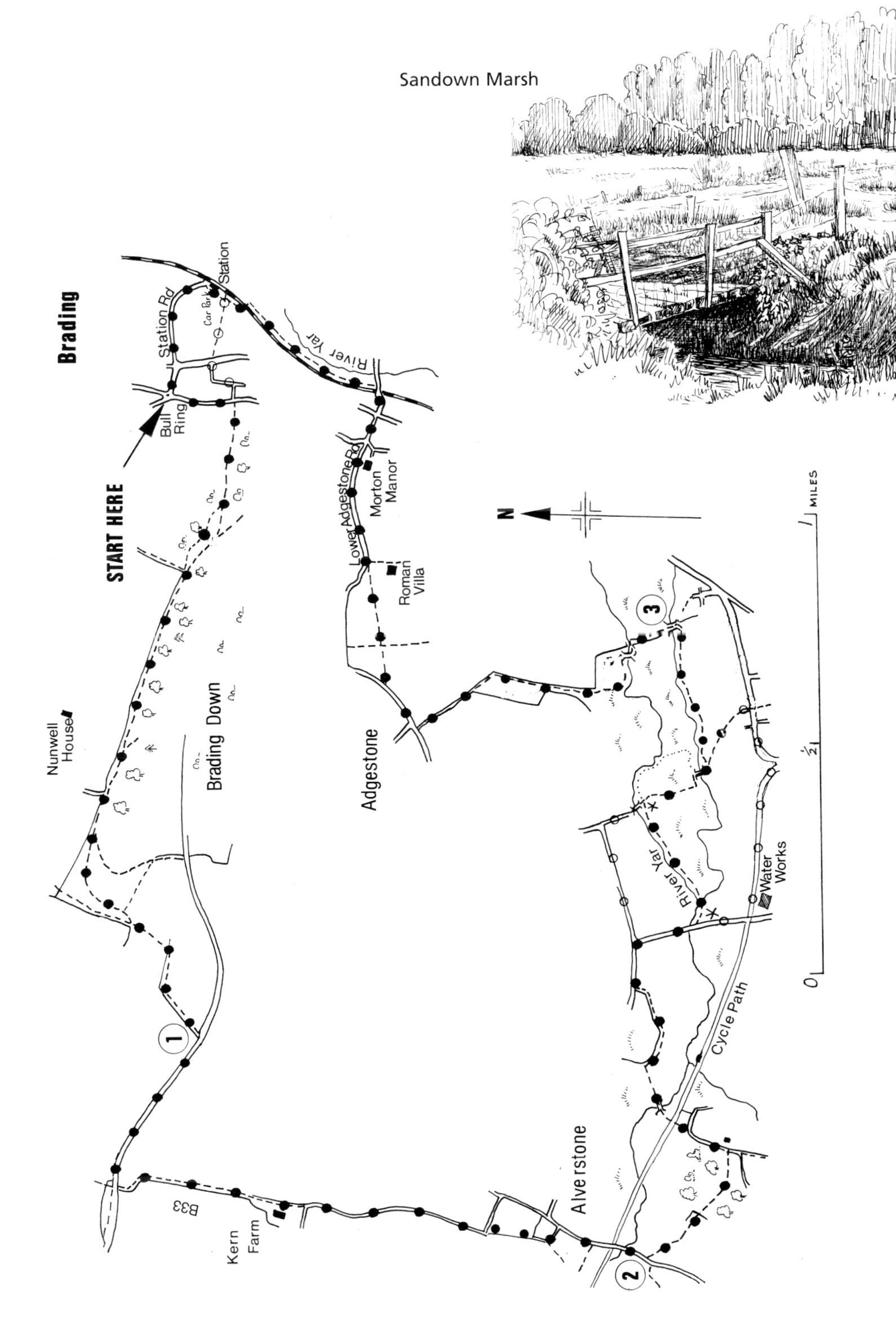

Sandown Marsh

11 Shanklin, Borthwood and America Wood *5½ miles*

Attractive areas of woodland are linked by field paths and tracks. The walk starts at Shanklin station. Grid Ref. 581819.

Please observe the country code, in particular keep to the footpaths, keep dogs under close control, and leave all wild flowers for others to enjoy.

Coming out of the station turn immediately right and passing parking bays, go down the steps to the road. Go right to the bend and cross to bridleway SS18. In Lower Hyde Leisure Park bear right and on reaching SS17 bear right again through the gate.

Where the track crosses a lane turn left on SS18a. Keep on the metalled track to Ninham Farm where you go down right to walk between the ponds. Cross the stream and turn right on SS20 towards Scotchells Bridge.

When you reach the road the path exits up some steps. Take care as there is no pavement on this side of the road. Cross over and go left along the pavement turning right to walk along the entrance to the Isle of Wight Airport. (1)

Continue ahead on the track that crosses the end of the runway to climb the hill beside the caravan park. Passing a white house at the top walk between high hedges. Having passed some houses on your right turn left along a short footpath into Borthwood Copse.

Follow the path to the right. This path then turns to the left and at a crossing of paths go left towards a clearing under big beech trees. Passing these big trees on your left follow the main track up and then downhill through the wood. Where paths converge at the bottom bear left slightly uphill. This main bridleway leaves the wood by an electricity pole. (2)

Walk straight ahead across the field and continue beside the next field with the hedge on your left. Climbing to the corner turn right with the hedge on your left. Just past Bigbury Farm turn left across the access road to a narrow path with the hedge on your right.

At the end of this path cross the road to the path directly opposite. (3) This path goes through a narrow strip of woodland. At the end of the trees cross the track and climb the bank opposite. The path goes beside fields and then down steps into woodland. Follow the path over a bank presently bearing right to enter America Woods over a stile on your left.

In a few metres go through a barrier to a path by a stile and a gate. Go up to the right. The path continues beside a little valley down to your right. Crossing a bridge go left up towards a cottage. (4) Pass the back of the cottage on your left and continue uphill to climb a set of steps. A good track leads forward round the hill outside the wood.

This track descends between the barns and farmhouse of Upper Hyde. Continue downhill across the field. Across the stile the narrow path leads to the caravan park. Cross the main track to climb over the bridge and turn left to walk down the road. By a guide post on your left go down steps to walk beside the road to the station.

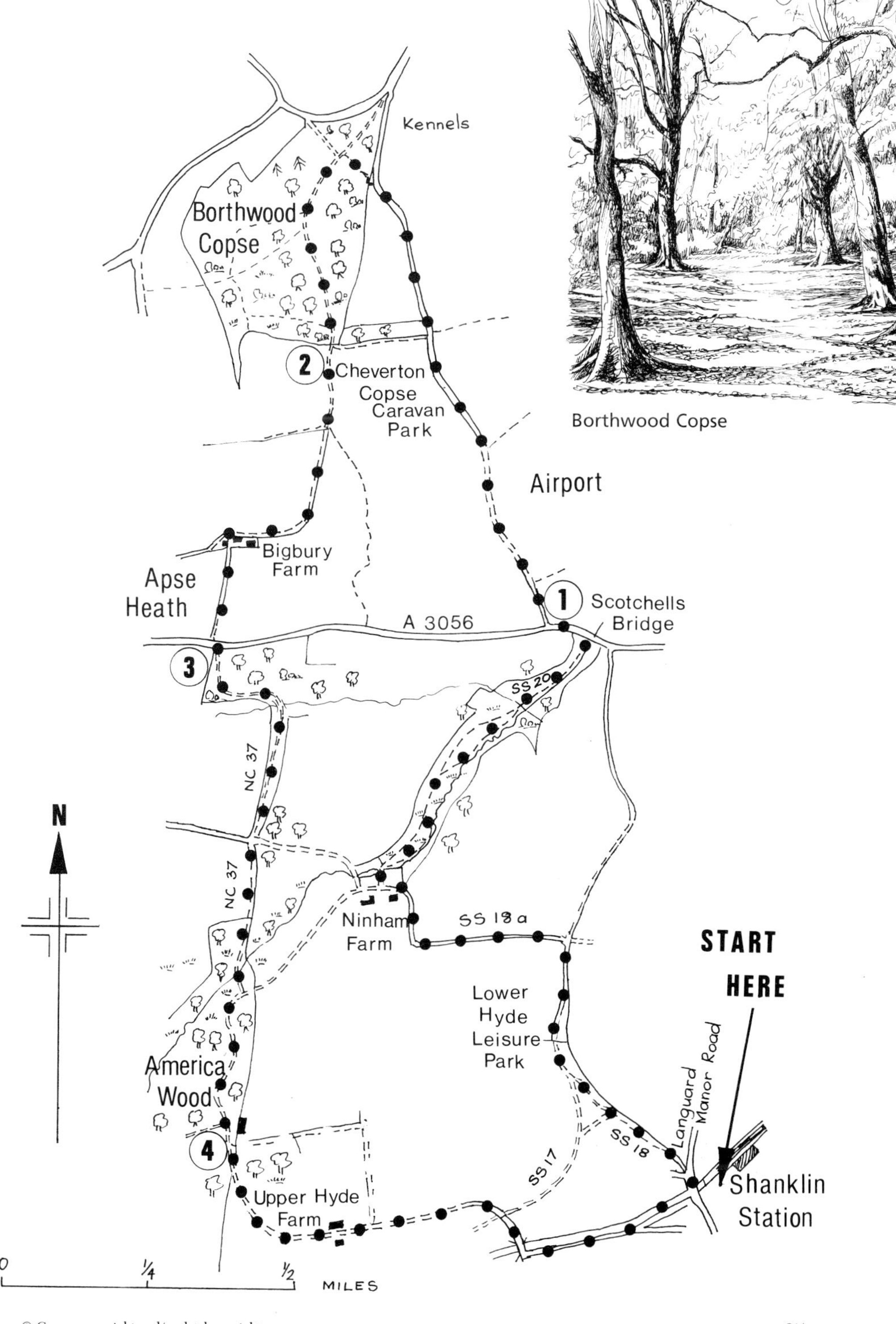

Borthwood Copse

12 Ventnor, St Boniface Down and Rew Down *8 miles*

Climbing from sea level to the top of Bonchurch Down this is quite a demanding walk. Continuing over Wroxall and Rew Downs the route returns to Ventnor along the Coastal Path. The walk starts on the sea front Grid Ref. 563773.

Please observe the country code, in particular keep to the footpaths, keep dogs under close control, and leave all wild flowers for others to enjoy.

From the town centre make your way to the sea front and walking with the sea on your right go along the sea wall. At Horseshoe Bay pass along Shore Road and after the first houses take the coast path steps up to the left.

Follow the path up past the old church and then the road past the entrance to East Dene. At the road junction go right uphill passing the parish church. Where the road bends right go along the road ahead called The Pitts. Look out for the footpath on your right which ascends abruptly up the Chimney Steps.(1)

Emerging onto Leeson Road go left to cross over to the footpath leading up onto the down. Through the kissing gate bear right and at the top of the steps go right on a path running along the side of the down.

Through a further kissing gate continue on round the down to meet a path coming up from the bend in the road. Turn left up this path to a stile.

Over the stile continue climbing with the scrub on your left and follow the path which climbs the centre of this hill. Continue along the ridge and bear left to a guide post. Go straight ahead here to walk below the radar station fence.

At the far corner turn right with the fence and when you reach the tarmac track go left. (2) Where this track bends left go straight ahead on the bridleway towards Wroxall. This curves gently right past gorse and descends to a bridle gate and guide post. Leave the bridleway and go diagonally left over the low brow. The path

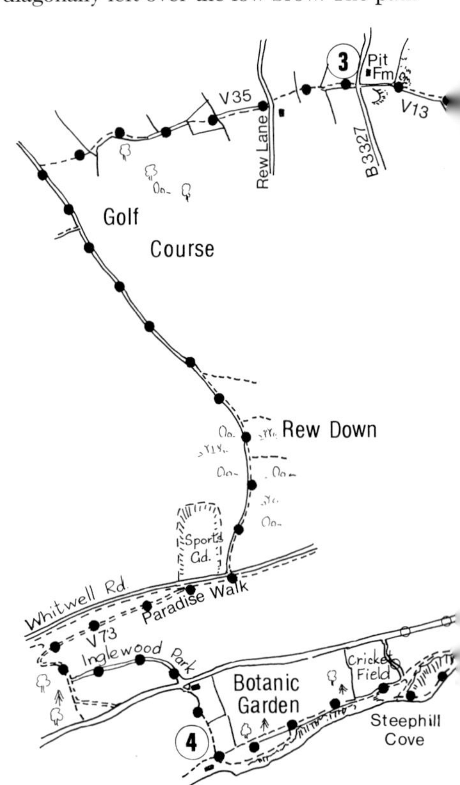

Coastal Path Near Ventnor

descends beside a hedge on your left and presently in the corner continues down to the road on an enclosed path.

Cross the road (3) into the right hand field. Follow the curving edge down passing an overgrown bottle tip on your left. At the bottom of the field continue down with the hedge on your right. Over the last stile go left on the lane to a footpath on your right. Climb the first field beside the hedge and through the gate head across the hollow to the multiple gates. The path climbs the track between fences (use the stile if muddy) to reach the trees. Turn right below the trees and follow the hedge to bend left and up to the stile.

Across the stile climb straight up over the golf course passing between two grass banks to reach a stile onto a bridleway. Go left and follow this path as it descends to the road beside a sports ground.

At the road there is a path beyond the hedge opposite. Go left a few yards to a gap in the hedge and then go right along the path. Where the path divides go down the left fork. At the bottom the path curves left to a residential road. Go left along this road and where it joins the main road cross to the footpath opposite.

This passes between farm buildings on a track and then becomes an enclosed path giving access to the Coastal Path.(4) Go left along the meadow, then keeping left follow the path inside the Botanic Gardens. At the far seaward corner of the garden continue on the Coastal Path to Ventnor via steps and Steephill Cove.

The path passes the La Falaise car park and descends to the esplanade.

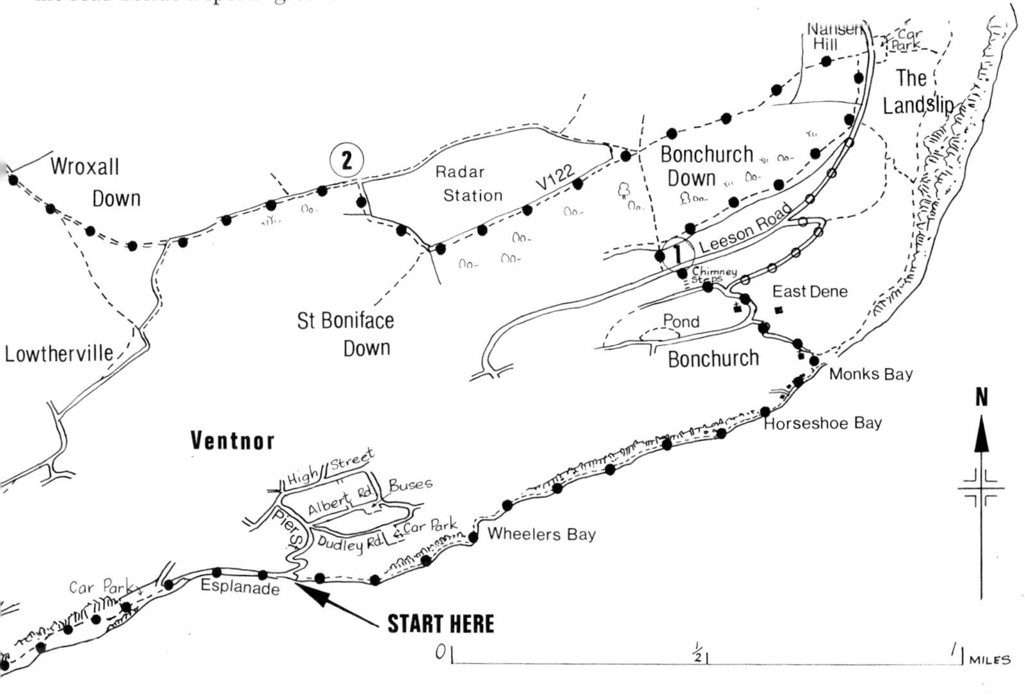